# THE KIDZ BIBLE

LEENA LANE
AND
GILLIAN CHAPMAN

# Contents

### THE OLD TESTAMENT

| | |
|---|---|
| 6 | In the beginning |
| 8 | Noah's ark |
| 10 | God's promise to Abraham |
| 11 | Rebecca's kindness |
| 12 | Jacob and Esau |
| 14 | Jacob's favourite son |
| 16 | Joseph in Egypt |
| 18 | The baby in the basket |
| 20 | The plagues of Egypt |
| 22 | Moses crosses the Red Sea |
| 23 | Joshua and the walls of Jericho |
| 24 | Gideon's victory |
| 25 | The strength of Samson |
| 26 | David plays for King Saul |
| 28 | David and Goliath |
| 30 | Elijah |
| 32 | Thrown to the lions! |
| 34 | Jonah and the big fish |

## The New Testament

| | |
|---|---|
| 36 | Jesus is born |
| 38 | The shepherds' surprise |
| 40 | Following the star |
| 42 | Jesus is baptised |
| 43 | The wedding at Cana |
| 44 | The soldier's servant |
| 45 | The terrible storm |
| 46 | The lost sheep |
| 47 | The lost coin |
| 48 | Jesus feeds the hungry crowd |
| 50 | The prodigal son |
| 52 | A welcome for the King |
| 53 | The last supper |
| 54 | Jesus is arrested |
| 56 | Jesus dies on a cross |
| 58 | 'Jesus is alive!' |
| 60 | Jesus' friends spread the good news |

# In the beginning

At the beginning of time, God made the light and the darkness.

God made big, tall mountains and deep blue seas.

God made plants and flowers and trees and filled the land with them.

God made the round, spinning earth, the red hot sun and the silvery moon. He made twinkling stars and planets.

God filled the sea with slippery, shiny fish and the air with birds that chatter and sing.

God filled the land with animals of every kind, tall and short, prickly and furry, striped and spotted and patterned.

'Now I will make people,' said God. God made Adam and Eve – a man and a woman who could think and feel and love. He wanted them to be His friends. He made a beautiful garden for them to live in called the Garden of Eden.

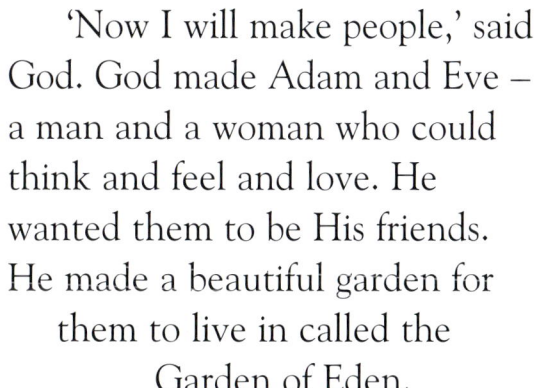

God was pleased with everything He had made. It was very good.

# Noah's ark

God had made a beautiful world, but it wasn't long before the people He had made began to spoil it. Adam and Eve did not do as God told them. They ate the fruit of a tree which God told them to leave alone. So they had to leave the Garden of Eden. Now there was trouble in the world which would not go away.

Soon there was only one good man left. His name was Noah.

God told Noah what He planned to do. He was going to send a great flood.

God told Noah to build a huge wooden boat called an ark and to fill it with two of every kind of animal on the earth. Noah covered it with tar to keep out the water. It would float on the waters until the flood was over.

Noah packed food for his family and all the animals. Then it began to rain.

It rained and rained for forty days and nights. The rivers burst into flood. But the ark floated on the waters. God kept Noah safe.

At last the rain stopped and dry land appeared. The ark came to rest on the mountains of Ararat. And God put a rainbow in the sky as a promise that there would never be a flood to cover the whole earth again.

9

# God's promise to Abraham

Abram was a good man who followed God's ways. He left his home to settle in a new land which God showed him. 'I will make your family into a great nation and I will bless you,' God told him.

The problem was, Abram and his wife Sarai could not have children. Without children, their family could not grow any bigger.

But one day God told Abram that he would have a son and a very large family.

'Look at the stars and try to count them,' said God. 'You will have as many people in your family as the number of stars you can see.'

Abram trusted God and believed His special promise.

Then, when Abram was ninety-nine years old, God's promise started to come true! God gave Abram and his wife new names – Abraham and Sarah. Sarah gave birth to a son. They were so happy, they named him 'Isaac', which means 'laughter'. God had kept His promise.

# Rebecca's kindness

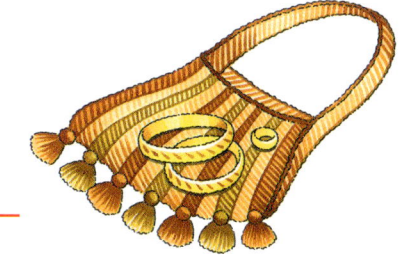

When Isaac grew up, Abraham sent a servant to his homeland to find a wife for Isaac. He took with him ten camels.

After a long hot journey, he stopped by a well to drink. He talked to God about his task: 'I will ask a girl to give me a drink. Let her be the one You want to marry Isaac.'

Late in the afternoon, Rebecca went to fetch water from the well for her family. She was very beautiful.

She noticed the servant standing at the well with his ten camels.

'Please give me a drink,' he said.

Rebecca offered him some water and then gave the camels a drink too. They were very thirsty.

Then the servant took a beautiful gold ring and gold bracelets out of his bag and put them on Rebecca. She had never seen anything so fine!

'Who is your father?' asked the servant. 'Is there room at your house for me and the camels to stay tonight?'

'My father's name is Bethuel,' said Rebecca. The servant knew that Bethuel was a relative of Abraham.

So they set off to see Rebecca's family.

That evening, the servant told Rebecca's father that he had come to find a wife for Abraham's son, Isaac. He asked if Rebecca would be Isaac's wife. She agreed and set off the next day to marry Isaac. They were very happy.

# Jacob and Esau

Isaac and Rebecca had twin boys called Esau and Jacob. They were very different!

Esau had red hair and was very hairy. He was a skilful hunter and loved being outdoors with his bow and arrows.

Jacob was a quiet man who liked staying at home with his mother, Rebecca. He loved cooking. He had a big cooking pot and made wonderful soups and stews in it for all the family.

Esau was born first, which meant that when his father died, Esau would be given all that his father owned and a special blessing. Jacob secretly wanted to be the one to get this, so he planned to trick his brother.

One day, when Esau came home from hunting, he was very hungry. He could smell a delicious stew that Jacob had been cooking. It was made of lentils and beans.

'Can I have some of that stew?' Esau asked Jacob.

'Only if you promise to let me be the one who gets Dad's special blessing,' said Jacob.

Esau couldn't resist the stew any longer, so he promised to let Jacob have their father's blessing and all he owned. Esau only cared about his hungry tummy!

Jacob was very pleased that his trick had worked.

When their father, Isaac, was very old and almost blind, Jacob pretended to be Esau and tricked his father into giving him the special blessing.

Esau was so angry, Jacob had to run away from home! It was many years before he saw his brother again. But when they met, Jacob was sorry for the tricks he had played. Esau forgave his brother and they became friends again.

# Jacob's favourite son

Jacob had a large family of twelve sons and one daughter.

Jacob loved all his children, but his favourite was Joseph.

When Joseph was seventeen years old, his father gave him a very special present. He gave him a wonderful coat to wear.

Joseph was very pleased with his coat and walked around proudly in front of his brothers. 'Look at me!' he said. 'Dad's given me this coat!'

But his brothers were jealous.

Why did their father love him more than he loved them?

Why couldn't they all have a splendid coat?

They didn't want Joseph to be more important than them.

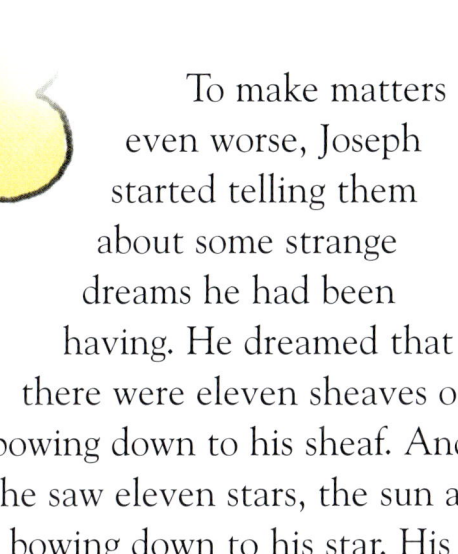

To make matters even worse, Joseph started telling them about some strange dreams he had been having. He dreamed that there were eleven sheaves of corn, all bowing down to his sheaf. And then he dreamed he saw eleven stars, the sun and the moon, all bowing down to his star. His brothers were furious.

One day when the brothers were in the fields looking after their father's sheep and goats, they decided what to do. When Joseph came to see them, the brothers threw him into an empty well! They were going to leave him there, but when they saw a group of travelling traders on their way to Egypt, the brothers decided to sell Joseph to the traders. So Joseph was taken to Egypt to be a slave.

The brothers thought they would never see Joseph again. But God had plans for Joseph.

# Joseph in Egypt

When Joseph arrived in Egypt, he was bought by the captain of the guard, Potiphar. Joseph worked hard for his new master. Potiphar was pleased with Joseph and soon put him in charge of his household.

But Potiphar's wife told lies about Joseph and he was thrown into prison.

In prison Joseph met the king's chief baker and the king's wine steward. They were prisoners too.

One night, they had unusual dreams. Joseph said he would try to help them understand what the dreams meant. The wine steward spoke first: 'I dreamt that there was a grapevine with three branches. The grapes ripened and I squeezed them into the king's cup and gave it to him to drink.'

Joseph said, 'In three days the king will let you out of prison and give you back your old job. Please remember me when you are out of prison and tell the king about me.'

Next it was the baker's turn: 'I was carrying three bread-baskets on my head. In the top basket were all sorts of pastries for the king, and the birds were eating them all up.'

Joseph told him: 'In three days the king will let you out of prison, but he will cut off your head.' The poor baker was very worried.

But it all happened just as Joseph had said. Two years later, the king began to have strange dreams which no one understood. The king's wine steward told the king about Joseph. Joseph told the king what his dreams meant. The king made Joseph into an important leader in Egypt. One day, Joseph's brothers came to Egypt to beg for help. There was no more food in their land and Egypt had plenty. They did not recognise their lost brother as the great man before them. When Joseph told them who he was, they said how sorry they were for what they had done.

Joseph was so pleased to see his brothers. He forgave them, and the whole family came to live in Egypt. They were all together again at last. God had looked after Joseph.

# The baby in the basket

While Joseph was alive, his family lived happily in Egypt. But after his death, new kings came who didn't know how God had blessed him. Joseph's children became slaves in Egypt. And the new king was a very cruel man.

Soon there were so many slaves that the king began to fear them. So he ordered all the baby boys to be thrown into the river and drowned.

But one woman had a clever plan. She hid her baby until he was three months old. Then she made a special basket out of reeds and covered it with tar to keep out the water. She put her baby in it and placed it in the bulrushes at the side of the river.

The baby's sister, Miriam, watched close by.

A little while later, the king's daughter came to the river to bathe. She saw the basket, heard a tiny noise and found the baby inside. The princess wanted to help him.

Miriam stepped out from the bulrushes.

'I know who can nurse the baby,' said Miriam. And she fetched her own mother.

The baby was called Moses and was looked after by his mother until he was old enough to live in the palace with the princess.

# The plagues of Egypt

When Moses grew up, he was upset to see how badly the cruel king treated his slaves. Moses ran away from the palace and became a shepherd in Midian.

One day, as Moses was looking after some sheep, he saw a strange sight. A bush appeared to be on fire, yet it did not burn up. Moses went to have a closer look. Suddenly, God spoke from the bush! 'Moses,' said God, 'I have heard My people crying out to Me for help. I have come to rescue them from the cruel Egyptians and take them to a new land of their own, flowing with milk and honey. I am sending you to bring My people out of Egypt.'

Moses was afraid, but God promised to help him. Moses went to the king of Egypt and told him to let God's people go. But the king would not listen. So Moses warned him that there would be terrible plagues.

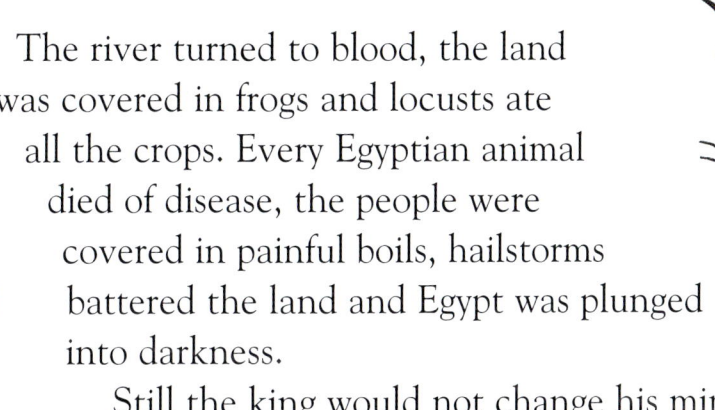

The river turned to blood, the land was covered in frogs and locusts ate all the crops. Every Egyptian animal died of disease, the people were covered in painful boils, hailstorms battered the land and Egypt was plunged into darkness.

Still the king would not change his mind. Finally, God sent the most terrible plague of all. The firstborn sons of Egypt would die, including the king's son. But God kept the Israelites safe. He told them to paint their doorposts with blood from a lamb, then eat a special meal of lamb, bitter herbs and bread without yeast.

'You must remember this night for ever,' said God. It was called Passover, when death passed over the houses of the Israelites and God kept them safe.

That night, the firstborn sons of Egypt were killed. The king's own son died.

'Go and leave Egypt!' the king said in despair.

So Moses led his people out of Egypt on a long journey towards a new land promised to them by God.

# Moses crosses the Red Sea

Moses set off to lead God's people out of Egypt. But suddenly the king changed his mind! He ordered the Egyptian army to follow them with chariots and horses.

Moses had camped with the people near the Red Sea. When they saw the army coming, they were terrified. But Moses said, 'Don't be afraid! God will help us.'

God told Moses to walk towards the Red Sea, with his stick held high.

A strong wind blew the water back and a path of dry ground appeared between two walls of water. Moses led his people across the path to safety on the other side of the Red Sea.

The Egyptian army tried to follow, but their chariot wheels got stuck in the ground. God told Moses to hold out his hand over the water again. The sea came crashing down over the Egyptian army. All the soldiers were drowned.

Moses led the people on towards the promised land.

But there were troubles ahead. They wandered in the wilderness for forty years.

God spoke to Moses many times. Moses taught the people to trust God, as God provided special food and drink for them every day. He gave Moses the Ten Commandments on stone tablets, telling the people how to live.

Moses himself never entered the promised land, but God showed him the land from a mountaintop before he died. He had been a brave and faithful leader.

# Joshua and the walls of Jericho

After Moses died, Joshua was chosen by God to lead God's people to the promised land. But first they had to get past the city of Jericho. The city had huge thick stone walls. It seemed impossible to get through. But God had a plan.

God told Joshua to choose seven priests with trumpets made of rams' horns. They must march round the city ahead of the people once every day for six days, blowing their trumpets, following the special Covenant Box which held the stone tablets which God had given to Moses.

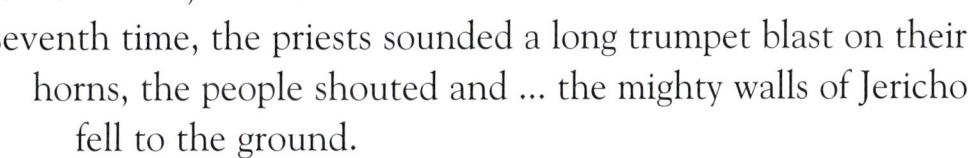

On the seventh day, the priests had to march round six times. Then, on the seventh time, the priests sounded a long trumpet blast on their horns, the people shouted and ... the mighty walls of Jericho fell to the ground.

God had given them the city.

# Gideon's victory

When Joshua died, the Israelite people began to turn away from God and His commandments. This made God angry. Armies from other countries came to fight against the Israelites. Finally, God sent judges to guide and help the Israelites. One of the judges was Gideon.

Gideon was chosen to lead the army. He knew that God was on his side and would help him defeat the Midianite army.

He gave each soldier a trumpet and a jar with a burning torch inside.

'This is what we must do,' he told his army. 'When I get to the edge of the camp, watch me and copy what I do. When I blow my trumpet, blow yours too and shout, "A sword for the Lord and for Gideon!"'

So Gideon and his men came to the edge of the camp in the middle of the night. They blew their trumpets and broke the jars they were holding.

Then everyone broke their jars, picked up their trumpets and shouted: 'A sword for the Lord and for Gideon!'

The enemy army ran away! God had helped Gideon win the battle.

# The strength of Samson

Even after all God had done for them, the Israelites turned away from God. So for forty years they were attacked by the fearsome Philistine army.

God sent another judge to the people to try and save the Israelites from the Philistines. He was called Samson.

Samson was a very, very strong man. He once fought a lion and killed it with his own hands! God had made him strong.

Nobody knew the secret of his great strength.

One day Samson met a woman called Delilah. The Philistines paid her to find out the secret of his strength.

Delilah kept on and on asking him until finally he could stand it no longer.

'If I cut off my hair, I will be made weak,' said Samson.

So, when Samson was asleep, Delilah called to his enemies and they cut off his hair. At once his strength left him. He was blinded and thrown into prison in chains.

But Samson's hair began to grow again …

The Philistines had a big party in the Temple because they had captured Samson. Samson prayed to God to give him his strength back one more time. With a mighty effort, he pushed over the pillars of the Temple.

The roof fell down and all his enemies were killed. Samson died with them.

# David plays for King Saul

The Israelites wanted a king. 'We want to have a king like all the other nations,' they said, 'someone to lead us in battle.' They asked a wise prophet called Samuel to find a king for them.

The first king of Israel was called Saul. Samuel anointed him as king by pouring oil over his head. 'Long live the king!' shouted the people.

At first Saul tried to be a good king and listened to God. He led his armies into battle against their enemies. But later Saul did not do as God told him and God became angry.

God told Samuel to go to Bethlehem and find the sons of Jesse. One of them, David, was anointed to be king after Saul's death.

King Saul had become a very troubled man since he had not done what God had told him to do. Now he often sat in his room feeling terrible.

His servants thought that it might help him to listen to some music. 'There is a boy in Bethlehem,' said one servant, 'who is very good at playing the harp. His name is David. He takes care of his father's sheep.'

Saul asked them to fetch David. Saul did not know that David had been anointed to be the next king.

David set off from home with a young goat, a donkey, food and drink.

He arrived at the king's tent and went to see the king, ready to play his harp.

King Saul listened to him playing the harp and suddenly felt much better. The music helped him to feel calm again.

'Stay here,' he said to David. 'I wish to hear more.'

So David stayed with the king. Whenever the king felt terrible, David would play beautiful music on his harp.

# David and Goliath

Who could fight a giant?

Goliath, the champion of the Philistine army, asked King Saul to find a man who would fight him. But Goliath was over three metres tall! No one in Saul's army even dared to try!

For forty days, Goliath asked the army, 'Who will fight me?'

Then, one day, David left his sheep to take some food to his brothers, who were soldiers in the camp.

David heard Goliath shouting. He couldn't understand why no one stepped forward. David had often fought wild animals to protect his sheep.

'God will help me fight Goliath,' said David, 'as He has helped me protect my sheep.'

'Then put on my armour and take my sword,' King Saul said. But they were much too heavy for David.

David had his own plan. He went to the river and chose five smooth stones. He took out his sling, then set off to face Goliath. With a quick flick of his wrist, he whirled the sling round his head and threw one of the stones at Goliath. It hit the giant on the forehead and killed him!

The Philistines turned and ran away, chased by King Saul's army. God had given the Israelites a victory!

Everyone loved David and called him a hero. This made King Saul very jealous. For the rest of his life, Saul tried to kill David.

But after Saul's death, David became king of Israel.

Israel grew into a mighty nation. David's son, Solomon, became the next king. He was very wise and built a magnificent temple for God.

# Elijah

After Solomon, many kings did not follow God's ways. One bad king was called Ahab.

King Ahab built a temple and altars for other gods called Baal. This made God very angry.

Elijah was a prophet. God gave him messages for the people. Elijah went to see the king.

'Ahab!' said Elijah. 'There is going to be a terrible drought for many years. The rain will only come when I give the word.'

Elijah was now in danger. Ahab and his wife were trying to kill all God's prophets. So God told Elijah to run to the east and hide in the Kerith Ravine.

God ordered ravens to bring Elijah bread and meat every morning and evening. Elijah drank the cool water from the brook in the ravine until it dried up.

Then God told Elijah to go to Zarephath, where a widow offered him all she had – a handful of flour in a jar and a little oil.

Elijah told the widow to go and make a small loaf of bread. 'God says the jar of flour and the jug of oil will never be empty until the day the rains come again!' said Elijah. This is exactly what happened.

After more than three years of drought, God told Elijah to return to see King Ahab.

Elijah spoke boldly: 'You have turned away from God and worshipped Baal instead. Well,

let's have a contest to see who is the true God. Bring all the prophets of Baal to Mount Carmel,' said Elijah.

'Get two bulls. The prophets of Baal will put one bull on their altar. I will put the other bull on the altar of the Lord. Then the prophets of Baal can call upon their gods, and I will call upon the Lord God to send fire to burn up the bulls. Whoever answers with fire is the true God.'

The prophets of Baal shouted all day long, but there was no fire. 'Shout louder!' said Elijah, 'Perhaps Baal is asleep!' But no fire came.

Then Elijah put the bull on the altar of the Lord. 'Now fill four large jars with water and pour it on top,' he said to the servants, 'Do it three times!' Soon the altar was soaked with water.

Elijah stepped forward and prayed: 'Oh Lord God, please answer me. Show these people that you are the real God. Turn them back to you again.'

Suddenly God sent fire to burn up the bull on the altar and all the water around it. Everyone bowed down, shouting, 'The Lord is God!'

'Go and eat and drink, Ahab!' said Elijah to the king. 'There is the sound of heavy rain.' A small raincloud appeared in the sky. Soon the rains fell again.

God had sent fire and rain and shown that He was the true God.

# Thrown to the lions!

Many kings later, King Nebuchadnezzar of Babylon came to Jerusalem and held it captive. He took away the king and treasures from the Temple of God. Nebuchadnezzar also commanded that some of Israel's handsome young men should come and serve in the royal household in Babylon. One of these men was called Daniel. Daniel was taken far away from his home.

He loved God and prayed to Him, but the people around him didn't like it. Daniel worked hard and the king made him a leader. But Daniel's enemies were jealous and plotted against him.

The king had made a rule that no one should pray to anyone but the king for thirty days, or they would be thrown into a pit of lions. When Daniel went on praying to God, he was arrested and taken to be fed to the lions!

The king was horrified but he hoped that Daniel would somehow survive.

As soon as morning came, he went back to the lions' pit and called, 'Daniel! Has your God saved you?'

Daniel called back, 'Yes! I'm alive!'

God had sent an angel to stop the lions from harming him.

The king released Daniel and punished the men who had tried to hurt him. The king commanded all his people to honour Daniel's God: 'He is the living God, who has rescued Daniel from the lions!'

So Daniel was free to pray to God for the rest of his life.

# Jonah and the big fish

God told Jonah to go to Nineveh and tell the people that God was angry with them. But Jonah was afraid! He went aboard a ship and set sail for a distant shore in the opposite direction. He was running away from God. But Jonah couldn't hide.

God sent a mighty storm, so bad that the sailors thought they would all drown.

'It's my fault!' said Jonah. 'I ran away from God! You must throw me into the sea!'

At first the sailors didn't want to throw Jonah overboard. But the storm became worse and they were in great danger. So they threw Jonah out of the boat.

The storm stopped as soon as Jonah sank down into the dark water.

But God saved Jonah from drowning.

He sent an enormous fish to come and swallow up Jonah.

Inside the fish, Jonah prayed to God. 'Thank You for saving me!' he prayed. 'You are a great God.'

Jonah stayed inside the fish for three days and three nights. It was very dark and smelly. Then the fish spat him out onto a beach.

'Now go to Nineveh!' said God. This time Jonah did as God had asked him.

By sending Jonah, God wanted to show His love for all the people of Nineveh. God gave them a chance to say sorry for all the wrong things they had done, and He forgave them.

# Jesus is born

God had promised to send a Saviour to His people. No one knew when He would come, but many people were waiting.

God sent the angel Gabriel to a town called Nazareth. He had come to tell Mary that God had chosen her for a very special purpose. She would have a baby called Jesus.

'Jesus will be very important. He will be called the Son of God!' said the angel. Mary sang praises to God for choosing her to be the mother of God's Son!

Mary was soon to be married to Joseph. Joseph's family came from Bethlehem.

Shortly before Mary's baby was due to be born, Joseph had to return to Bethlehem to be counted by the Roman governor. Mary had to go too.

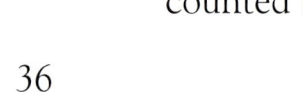

It was a very long, tiring journey. Joseph walked in front, with Mary a little way behind. Their donkey carried their small bundles of clothes and a water bottle.

When they arrived in Bethlehem, there was nowhere to stay! Mary was very tired, because her baby was soon to be born. Joseph knocked on many doors in the town, trying to find a room for them to sleep in that night. At last an innkeeper said they could stay near his inn where the animals slept. There was no bed, but it was warm and dry in the straw.

Jesus was born and Mary laid her new baby in a manger on the soft hay.

# The shepherds' surprise

On the hills near Bethlehem, a group of shepherds were looking after their sheep. It was night and they had to make sure that no wild animals came to snatch their sheep away. The shepherds camped round a fire to keep them warm. They began to feel a bit sleepy. Suddenly there was a blinding flash in the sky. An angel appeared!

'Don't be afraid!' he said. 'I have come to bring you good news. This very night a baby has been born in Bethlehem. He is Christ the Lord! You will find the baby wrapped in strips of cloth and lying in a manger. Go now and see Him!'

The shepherds could not speak – they were very frightened and amazed.

Then a whole host of angels appeared in the sky, singing, 'Glory to God in the highest, and on earth peace to men!' It was a beautiful sound.

'Hurry, hurry!' shouted the shepherds. 'We must go to Bethlehem at once to find the baby which God has told us about!'

They hurried through the town, looking for a newborn baby. They knocked at the door of an inn. 'Is there a baby here?' they asked the inn-keeper. The inn-keeper showed the shepherds through to the back of the house, where the animals slept. And here they found Mary and Joseph.

There, in a manger, wrapped up in cloths, was the new-born baby: Jesus, their Saviour. The shepherds looked at the tiny baby and they felt great joy in their hearts.

When they had said goodbye, they hurried into the town, telling everyone they met, 'We've seen Jesus!' They danced and sang songs to God, praising Him for all they had seen. It had been just as the angel had said.

# Following the star

**W**hen Jesus was born in Bethlehem, wise men in lands far away spotted a very bright star in the sky.

They thought it meant that a new king had been born. So they set off with gifts and followed the star.

On their way, the wise men came to King Herod's palace.

'Do you know where the new king has been born?' they asked.

King Herod did not want there to be another king in the land. He was jealous. He asked the wise men to find Jesus, then return and tell him all about it.

The wise men followed the star all the way to Bethlehem, where they found Jesus with His mother Mary. They gave Jesus special gifts of gold, frankincense and myrrh.

God warned the wise men in a dream not to go back to King Herod, so they went home by a different road. And God warned Joseph to take Mary and the baby Jesus to Egypt, where they would be safe from King Herod.

# Jesus is baptised

There was a man called John the Baptist who talked to people about God. He told them to say sorry for the wrong things they had done. Then John baptised them in the water of the River Jordan as a sign of God washing their sins away.

When Jesus was about thirty years old, He came to see John on the bank of the river.

'I want you to baptise Me in the river,' said Jesus.

John was very surprised. He knew that Jesus was special, and that He had come to show people God's love. But he also knew that Jesus had done nothing wrong and didn't need to be baptised.

When Jesus came out of the river, He saw a dove, and a voice from heaven spoke: 'This is My Son, with whom I am pleased.' It was God's voice speaking.

Jesus began to travel around, telling people about God. He did many amazing things, called miracles.

Jesus chose twelve disciples to be His special friends.

# The wedding at Cana

Jesus was invited to a wedding at Cana in Galilee. There was a great feast and everyone was enjoying the party. Then suddenly the wine began to run out.

'You must do something,' said Mary, Jesus' mother. But Jesus knew what God wanted Him to do. He told the servant to fill six large stone jars with water, then take them to the man in charge of the feast. When the man tasted it, he was very pleased.

'That's funny!' said the man. 'People usually serve the best wine first, but you have left the best wine till last!' He didn't know that Jesus had done an amazing miracle.

Jesus had turned the water into wine!

# The soldier's servant

Jesus did many amazing things. He healed people who were sick and made blind people see again. Crowds followed Him wherever He went. Jesus cared about all the people who came to Him.

One day, a Roman officer begged Jesus for help.

'My servant is very ill. He is too ill to leave the house.'

Jesus replied, 'I will go and make him well.'

'No, no,' said the officer. 'I know that if You just say the word, he will be healed. I trust that You will heal him.'

Jesus was surprised to hear this and was pleased to find that the officer trusted Him.

'Go home, then,' said Jesus. 'What you believe will be done.'

The officer ran home and found to his great joy that his servant had been made well again!

# The terrible storm

One day, Jesus and His friends got into a boat on the lake. It had been a very busy day and Jesus was tired.

Suddenly a fierce storm blew up and the boat was rocked about like a cork.

Jesus' friends were terrified of sinking, but Jesus was fast asleep in the boat.

'Save us, Lord!' they shouted to Jesus.

'Why are you so afraid?' said Jesus, waking up.

Then Jesus got up and ordered the wind and the waves to calm down.

The storm vanished. Everyone was amazed! 'Even the winds and the waves obey Him!' they said.

Jesus had saved them all from the storm on the lake.

# The lost sheep

Jesus once told a story about a shepherd.

'A shepherd had a hundred sheep. He looked after them all and protected them from wild animals.

One day he found that one was missing. So the shepherd set out to find his lost sheep, leaving the ninety-nine other sheep in the sheepfold.

He looked high and low, behind bushes and rocks. Where could the sheep be?

Suddenly the shepherd heard faint bleating; at last he had found his lost sheep!

He picked it up lovingly and carried it home on his shoulders.

He was so pleased to have found his lost sheep that he invited all his neighbours to a party.'

'God is like that shepherd,' said Jesus. 'He cares even if only one of His sheep is lost.'

# The lost coin

Jesus told another story, about a woman who had ten coins that were very special to her.

'One day the woman lost one of her coins. Her house was dark. The floor was dark. But she tried to find the missing coin.

She lit a lamp, swept her house and looked everywhere for it.

Suddenly she saw something shiny. There was the coin, hiding in a dark corner.

The woman called to her friends and neighbours and said, "Let's have a party! I am so happy to have found my lost coin!"'

'In the same way,' said Jesus, 'God is very pleased when anybody turns to follow Him. Each one is special, just like the woman's lost coin. God wants to keep each one safe.'

# Jesus feeds the hungry crowd

Jesus was once speaking to a large crowd of people. There were men, women and children too. They had been listening to Him all day and were getting hungry.

Jesus' friends thought the people should go away and buy some food, but Jesus wanted to feed them.

'Where can we buy food for all these people?' He asked His friends.

Philip replied, 'We would need more than two hundred silver coins to buy enough!'

Another of Jesus' friends, Andrew, said, 'There is a boy who says he will share his lunch. But he has only five loaves and two small fish.'

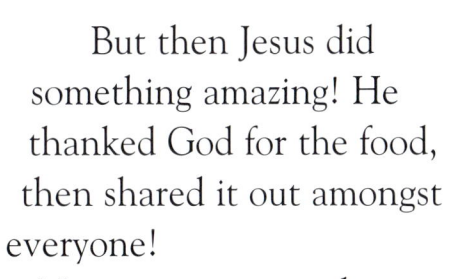

But then Jesus did something amazing! He thanked God for the food, then shared it out amongst everyone!

No one went away hungry. Jesus gave them all enough to eat, and there were even twelve baskets full of leftovers.

# The prodigal son

Jesus once told this story to explain how much God loves us:

'There was a boy who lived on a farm with his family. He grew bored of the countryside and had heard that the city was an exciting place. He wanted to go there. So he asked his dad for his share of his riches, and set off.

His father was very sad that his son had gone away. He loved his son very much and hoped he would come home.

Meanwhile, the son spent all the money very quickly, going to parties every night and having a great time. But when the money ran out, nobody wanted to be his friend any more. He had to find a job, feeding pigs. There was no food for him to eat, so he nearly ate the pig's food.

"I must go home," he thought. "Perhaps Dad will let me work on his farm."

As he came near to his old home, he saw his dad running towards him. He was shouting, "Welcome home!" and he reached out his arms to give him a great big hug.

The father gave a great party for his son. He thought he had lost him, but the son he loved had come back. How happy that made him!'

# A welcome for the King

Many people loved Jesus, but others were jealous of Him. They did not like the way crowds followed Him everywhere.

It was soon time for the Passover festival. Jesus spent a few days with His friends Mary, Martha and Lazarus in Bethany.

Then, on the first day of the week, Jesus set off to the great city of Jerusalem.

Clip, clop, clip, clop, went the donkey's hooves on the road.

'Hosanna! Hurray!' shouted the crowd.

Who was this, riding on a donkey? It was Jesus!

The people were so excited to see Him that they threw down cloaks in front of the donkey and waved palm branches in the air.

'God bless the King!' they shouted.

Jesus was welcomed into the city of Jerusalem. He was the King who had come to save His people.

# The last supper

Jesus knew that He would not be with His friends for much longer. He wanted to celebrate the Passover meal with them one last time. It was a special time of remembering how God had rescued Moses and the Israelites in Egypt many years ago.

Jesus met His twelve friends at the upper room of a house in Jerusalem.

Jesus took a bowl of water and began to wash His friends' feet.

'You mustn't wash my feet!' said Peter. 'You are our Master, not our servant!'

'Unless I wash you, you don't belong to Me,' said Jesus. 'Then wash my hands and head as well!' said Peter.

They reclined at the table. The meal was lamb, bread without yeast, bitter herbs and wine.

Jesus looked at His friends gathered round Him and said, 'One of you is going to hand Me over to be killed.'

'Surely not I!' they all said. Jesus already knew it would be Judas.

While they were eating, Jesus took the bread, broke it and gave it to His friends.

'Eat this and remember Me,' said Jesus. 'This is My body.'

Then He took the cup of wine, thanked God for it and handed it round.

'This is My blood, given for many,' said Jesus. 'Drink this and remember Me.'

# Jesus is arrested

Jesus knew that the time was coming for Him to be taken away. He asked His friends to come and pray with Him in the Garden of Gethsemane. But they kept falling asleep.

'Why are you sleeping?' he asked them. 'Watch and pray with Me.'

Suddenly a crowd came towards them, and Judas Iscariot was with them. There were soldiers and chief priests. Judas came near to Jesus to kiss Him. This showed the soldiers where Jesus was. They arrested Jesus and took Him away.

Jesus' other friends were very upset and alarmed, especially Peter. Earlier that evening, Jesus had warned Peter:

'Before the cock crows tonight, you will say three times that you do not know Me.'

Peter had been very upset. Jesus was his friend! Peter wouldn't let Him down.

But while Peter was waiting to see what would happen to Jesus, some girls came up to him and asked if he was a friend of Jesus.

'No,' said Peter, 'I don't know what you are talking about!'

They asked him three times and each time he said, 'No!'

Then suddenly a cock crowed. Peter remembered what Jesus had said. Peter felt terrible and cried bitterly. He had wanted to be a good friend to Jesus, but now he really had let Jesus down.

# Jesus dies on a cross

The soldiers who were guarding Jesus were very cruel to Him. Then Jesus was brought before Pilate, the Roman governor. 'What has this man done wrong?' Pilate asked the crowd.

'He is causing trouble all over the country,' said the chief priests. 'He says He is a king.'

'Are you the King of the Jews?' asked Pilate. 'Yes, it is as you say,' said Jesus.

'What shall I do with Jesus?' asked Pilate.

'Put Him on a cross to die!' shouted the crowd.

Pilate did not think Jesus had done anything wrong, but he wanted to please the crowd.

So he handed Jesus over to the soldiers to be killed. The soldiers put a purple robe on Him and a crown of thorns on His head.

Jesus was taken by the soldiers to a place called Golgotha. There He was nailed to a cross. Above His head was a sign saying: The King of the Jews.

It was a terrible day. Jesus' mother, Mary, stood close by and watched. How could they do this to her precious Son?

Darkness covered the land. At the ninth hour, Jesus cried out in a loud voice to God, then breathed His last breath. Jesus died.

His body was taken down from the cross and placed in a tomb belonging to Joseph of Arimathea.

Jesus' friends thought they would never see Him again.

# 'Jesus is alive!'

It was three days since Jesus had died on the cross. All His friends were heartbroken and didn't know what to do next.

Some of the women went to His tomb early on Sunday morning, but they had a shock! The large stone which blocked the entrance to the tomb had been rolled away!

They peered inside the dark tomb. Jesus' body had gone! All they could see were strips of cloth which the body had been wrapped in.

Suddenly two men in bright shining clothes appeared.

'Don't look for Jesus here,' they said. 'He's alive!'

The women couldn't believe it! They ran home as fast as they could and told Jesus' friends.

Very soon they all saw Jesus again for themselves. It was true! Jesus was alive!

Over the next forty days, Jesus appeared to His friends and talked to them about the coming of God's kingdom. He ate and drank with them. 'Don't leave Jerusalem,' said Jesus, 'but wait for the gift which God has promised to give you – the Holy Spirit. When He comes, you will be able to tell the whole world about Me!'

Then Jesus was taken up to heaven to be with God. A cloud hid Him from their eyes.

Suddenly two men in white clothes stood beside Jesus' friends. 'Why are you looking at the sky?' they asked. 'Jesus will return one day, in the same way as you saw Him go!'

# Jesus' friends spread the good news

Jesus' friends met together to pray every day. They chose a man called Matthias to replace Judas.

A few days later, on the Day of Pentecost, all of Jesus' friends met together in one place.

Suddenly there was a noise which sounded like a strong wind blowing. The noise filled the whole house. Then tongues of fire seemed to reach out and touch everyone in the room. Everyone was filled with the Holy Spirit and could suddenly speak all kinds of different languages!

There were people in Jerusalem from every country in the world, but they could all understand Jesus' friends in their own language.

Then Peter stood up and told them all about Jesus – how He had come to show God's power and do amazing things, how He had been put to death on a cross, then how God had made Him come alive again.

'Stop doing wrong and ask God to forgive you,' said Peter. 'Be baptised in the Name of Jesus and you will be given the Holy Spirit.'

That day, three thousand people asked to join the group of Jesus' friends!

Jesus' friends and everyone who believed in Jesus met together regularly. They prayed and ate together.

They shared everything they had and thanked God for their homes and food. The followers of Jesus were the first Christians. Jesus' friends were also able to do miracles and they healed the sick. They started to tell everyone about God.

But some people didn't want to listen. There was a man called Saul who hated Jesus' friends. He wanted them all to be captured or killed. But God had plans for Saul. One day, as Saul was travelling to Damascus, Jesus spoke to him from heaven. Saul was blinded by a bright light. Jesus told him to go to Damascus, where a Christian called Ananias was able to make him see again.

Saul changed completely. He no longer wanted to kill the Christians. In fact, he wanted to tell people about Jesus too! Saul was given a new name – Paul. He travelled far and wide, telling people about Jesus.

Jesus' followers were often in danger. But God helped them not to be afraid. They wanted people all over the world to know the amazing good news: that God loved the world so much that He sent His Son, Jesus, to save His people.

# Where to find the stories in the Bible

| | | |
|---|---|---|
| 6 | In the beginning | Genesis 1–2 |
| 8 | Noah's ark | Genesis 3; 6:5–8:22 |
| 10 | God's promise to Abraham | Genesis 12:1–3; 15:1–6; 21:1–6 |
| 11 | Rebecca's Kindness | Genesis 24 |
| 12 | Jacob and Esau | Genesis 25:19–34; 27; 33:1–4 |
| 14 | Jacob's favourite son | Genesis 37 |
| 16 | Joseph in Egypt | Genesis 39–47 |
| 18 | The baby in the basket | Exodus 2:1–10 |
| 20 | The plagues of Egypt | Exodus 3–12 |
| 22 | Moses crosses the Red Sea | Exodus 13:17–14:31; 16–20; Deuteronomy 34:1–2 |
| 23 | Joshua and the walls of Jericho | Joshua 1; 6 |
| 24 | Gideon's victory | Judges 6–7 |
| 25 | The strength of Samson | Judges 13–16 |
| 26 | David plays for King Saul | 1 Samuel 8–10; 16 |
| 28 | David and Goliath | 1 Samuel 17–19; 2 Samuel 5:1–5; 1 Kings 1:28–6:38 |
| 30 | Elijah | 1 Kings 16:29–18:46 |
| 32 | Thrown to the lions! | Daniel 1; 6 |
| 34 | Jonah and the big fish | Jonah 1–3 |
| 36 | Jesus is born | Matthew 1:18–24; Luke 1:26–38; 2:1–7 |
| 38 | The shepherds' surprise | Luke 2:8–20 |
| 40 | Following the star | Matthew 2:1–12 |
| 42 | Jesus is baptised | Matthew 3:13–17; Mark 1:9–11; Luke 3:21–22; John 1:31–34 |
| 43 | The wedding at Cana | John 2:1–11 |
| 44 | The soldier's servant | Matthew 8:5–13 |
| 45 | The terrible storm | Matthew 8:23–27 |
| 46 | The lost sheep | Matthew 18:10–14; Luke 15:1–7 |
| 47 | The lost coin | Luke 15:8–10 |
| 48 | Jesus feeds the hungry crowd | Matthew 14:13–21; Mark 6:30–44; Luke 9:10–17; John 6:5–13 |
| 50 | The prodigal son | Luke 15:11–31 |
| 52 | A welcome for the King | Matthew 21:1–11; Mark 11:1–10; Luke 19:29–38; John 12:12–15 |
| 53 | The last supper | Matthew 26:17–30; Mark 14:12–26; Luke 22:7–23; John 13:1–30 |
| 54 | Jesus is arrested | Matthew 26:31–75; Mark 14:27–72; Luke 22:47–62; John 18:1–27 |
| 56 | Jesus dies on a cross | Matthew 27:11–60; Mark 15:1–46; Luke 23:1–53; John 18:28–19:42 |
| 58 | 'Jesus is alive!' | Matthew 28; Mark 16:1–20; Luke 24; John 20; Acts 1:1–11 |
| 60 | Jesus' friends spread the good news | Acts 1:12–2:47; 5:12–16; 9:1–19 |